THE MORE YOU KNOW

A Safety Guide for Kids and Teens

How to Be Safe Anytime and Everywhere.

THE MORE YOU KNOW

A Safety Guide for Kids and Teens

How to Be Safe Anytime and Everywhere.

ISBN 979-8-3306-0744-0

Printed in the U.S.A

First OhMG Printing , December 2024

Safety Overview

What is Safety? 

Safety is more than just preventing cuts and scrapes. Safety is really just another word for protection. You are special and have so much to protect. But how? You need to take care of your body, mind, and emotions, so read on to learn how!

Ways to Be Safe

Make good decisions no matter where you are and what you are doing. This book will teach you all about keeping yourself safe. We will cover the following topics: internet safety, school safety, home safety, safe adults, safety with friends, safety at the doctor, safety in the big world, safety with your sitter and much more!

Internet Safety

Most kids have access to electronic devices on a daily basis. Whether it is a tablet, phone, laptop, or desktop computer, kids connecting to the internet is a normal daily occurrence. The internet is called the World Wide Web. It is exactly what it sounds like. It is a huge web of connections that

span across the entire world!! When you "get online" on your device, you are entering the real world, filled with strangers and dangers. It is very important to follow safety guidelines when taking such a large step into the world!

When you step outside, you'll see signs alerting you to road curves or safe crossing areas. These precautions help you make smart choices to stay safe.

When you click into the internet and enter the world wide web, there are no warning signs or signals to show you an upcoming danger. You may be in a dangerous place online and not even know it. It is an endless space of dangers and strangers and there are not warning signs as you move through it. How can you stay safe, then? Protect yourself with knowledge! The more you know, the better!

Here are some safety tips to keep you safe from harmful people on the internet:

Always ask a parent/guardian before going online. It is always safest to go online with a parent helping you. If they cannot be available to sit with you, make sure you have their permission to enter the internet. Don't hesitate to ask for their help as you travel the world wide web.

2. **Never give personal information!**

   Personal information includes things like: the town where you live, your school, your address, phone number, email address, parents' names, your name, etc. Any information you give can be found by anyone, even mean people who may use it to hurt you.

3. **Never enter a chat room, or chat on an online game.**

   It may seem harmless to chat as you are playing online games like ROBLOX. It isn't. There are adults, who pretend to be kids, lurking in the game, waiting for personal information to be leaked so they can find their next victim. Don't be a victim!

4. **Don't sign up for social media account unless you have your parents' permission and help.**

   If your parents approve of you having a social media account, they need to sign up for you, so your personal information isn't used. There are many privacy settings that need to be activated to keep you safe. Your parent needs to help you create a safe account. It is recommended that you make an account under a name nickname, so your real information isn't floating around the world of strangers.

Don't post any pictures or videos of yourself on social media.

It may seem harmless to take selfies and videos and show them off to friends on the social media pages. These photos and videos can be found by anyone! There are many bad adults who sift through social media and save images of children to use for bad purposes. It is scary, too, that many images have locations attached to the photo information. If a stranger saves you photo from social media, many times they can right click on it and find out the time, date, and location the image was taken—which could lead a stranger with bad intentions straight to your location!

If you are playing a game and a window pops up asking you to download another game, DON'T!

Pop-up windows and images are called "Click bait" –they bait you into clicking on their image by showing interesting, entertaining and eye appealing images. However, clicking on their links can lead you to harmful sites, with scary people that are stealing data from your computer, including your personal information and location. These links can also make your computer sick by leaving viruses. Viruses are like leeches. They sit inside your computer and absorb information about you and eventually shut your computer down.

7. **Don't accept friend requests from strangers on gaming sites.**

It is ok to accept friend requests on a gaming site if you know your real friend's username. It is not o.k. to accept friend requests from usernames of people you don't know in real life. For instance, if your friend Suzy tells you at school that her username is SuzyQ10 and you receive a friend request later from SuzyQ10, you can accept the friend request because you know SuzyQ10 is your friend Suzy from school. Whom you know in real life. BUT, if you get a friend request from ARTY9ER, and you were not told by any of your friends that this is them, then reject that request because you don't know that person in real life.

8. **When you are playing online games, whatever you write can be seen by everyone, not just friends.**

If you are playing a game like Roblox, and your friend is on your server, you may get an urge to write to them in the chat box. Whatever you write shows up in the speaking bubble and you and your friend can see it. HOWEVER, all the other people on that server can see it too.   No information is safe on the internet, even if you think only you and your friend see it.

People aren't always who they say.

It cannot be stressed enough how scary of a place the internet can be. Don't trust anybody online, even if they say they are a kid your age and seem cool. It is difficult to believe, but many adults go on the internet looking for child victims. They find these victims by sounding like a kid. They talk like a kid and talk about things that you think you have in common. They do this to gain your trust. When you think you made a friend, they may ask to meet you in person. DON'T MEET ANYONE! Tell a safe adult!

. **Don't ever agree to meet anyone in person that you met online. EVER!!!**

There are mean people who the world who prey on children. They gain their trust and meet them and grab them.   Those children become victims of child crimes, missing kids, and sometimes end up deceased.   Internet safety is nothing to take lightly. It can mean life and death.

11

What sounds like nagging from parents is just your parents loving you and wanting what is best for you—a safe, happy life!

WHO YOU THINK YOU ARE CHATTING WITH

WHO YOU REALLY ARE CHATTING WITH

11. Don't do online challenges!!

Online challenges are the trendy thing to do but did you know that you can harm yourself or even die when you do these so called "challenges"? There are some pretty crazy challenges online. For some reason, people think tey become invincible if they do something harmful in front of a camera. No matter what-nobody is invincible!

 in*vin*ci*ble *adjective*\(ˈ)in-ˈvin(t)-sə-bəl\ incapable of being defeated, overcome, or subdued (https://kids.britannica.com/kids/search/dictionary?query=invincible)

There are too many online challenges to list and this scary trend is growing every day. The important thing is to not follow the trend. These trends can lead to a deathly trend, and who wants to be a part of that? Don't take physical risks just because someone is pressuring you to, or telling you that you are not cool if you don't. You are actually a cool leader if you do not take part in these challenges. Be a leader and pave a new path—a safe path. Eating chemicals, catching yourself on fire, snorting items up your nose, placing bags over your head, choking yourself, getting duct-taped to something, burning yourself with ice and salt, and any other bad choice will hurt you--whether

or not you are on camera or home alone. DON'T do any of
these, or any new challenges that may occur.

School Safety

You go to school almost every day! Most of your life is
spent in school! It is important to make good choices and
stay safe while you are at school! Here are some
important guidelines to follow.

1. **If anyone is bullying you, tell safe adults!**

    Tell your parents, teacher, principal, or anyone you trust.
    Bullying is not a tolerable action. If anyone is bullying you,
    you need to get help. Bullies start small-one child—but
    they can also grow into more serous actions if they are not
    stopped. If a bully gets away with their actions, their
    actions may grow and eventually lead to harming many
    people. Violence is not ok. If you feel unsafe around
    someone, report it.

2. **If anyone makes you uncomfortable with words or a
    touch, tell safe adults!**

    A safe adult is anyone you are comfortable around. They
    can be a teacher, coach, principal, parent, or anyone that
    won't harm you.   HOWEVER, it is important to know that

not all teachers, parents, coaches, and principals are safe adults. Many people abuse their positions and gain the trust of kids and end up hurting them. If a person makes you uncomfortable, no matter their job title or position, report it to someone you trust! Just because they are an adult or work in a school, it doesn't automatically make them safe. They may be the subject of your report. Don't ever be alone in a room with an adult—always bring a friend, or another safe adult. If a teacher, coach, or another adult tries to get you alone, don't let them and tell a safe adult immediately.

Don't judge a book by the cover. Even predators can look safe.

THIS COULD BE A PREDATOR! ANYONE COULD BE A PREDATOR. Predators don't have a certain "look". A predator is spotted by actions, not outward appearances.

3. **Don't accept random gifts from teachers, coaches, or other people.**

There is an entire classroom of kids. If your teacher or coach tries to get you alone and gives you random gifts a lot, tell an adult. It may seem cool or make you feel special, but it is a trick to make you trust them before they use you as their prey and make you the next victim. Also, if an adult tries to let you do things that your parent won't normally let you do—be warned! Don't do the actions! Like, if a coach gets you alone and tells you its ok to look at dirty magazines—it isn't ok. Run and tell a safe adult. Remember, not all adults are safe.

STOP AND THINK, "THIS ISN'T SAFE!"

Be aware of bathrooms.

It seems harmless, you leave the classroom to use the restroom. You are alone in the stall when an adult enters the room. Stay safe in that stall until the adult leaves the bathroom. If the adult tries to make you uncomfortable— report it to a safe adult.

If you hear a student, or an adult, make a threat—report it!

Sometimes, we hear things that scare us. If you hear people talking about hurting themselves, another student, or threatening the safety of the entire school—report it!! If a student tells you something that will harm themselves or others and tells you not to say anything—report it!! It is good to gain the trust of a friend by keeping secrets, but not at the expense of safety! Secrets need told if they threaten the safety of anyone involved. Your report may save the life of one or lives of many!

Don't take candy from just anyone—even at school!

This sounds silly. I mean it's just candy, right? WRONG! It's sad, but there are people out there that disguise drugs as candy to try and get young kids addicted! Even if you see a candy that looks normal, it could be laced with scary

drugs!

The image below shows how people take sour patch kids

and lace them with LSD—a serious drug that causes

hallucinations and even death. There are many candies

out there that are either laced with drugs, or are pure

drugs made to look like candy.

Many gummy bears, sour candies, Sweet Tarts, and more

are deadly if in the wrong hands

Candy being laced with a drug called LSD.

No candy is worth risking your life

over. Not everyone can be trusted.

LSD.https://www.reddit.com/r/LSD/comments/230sx5/sour_patch_trips/

Home Safety

Home is where you feel comfortable! Ah, I'm home. I'm going to kick off my shoes and relax! Great! We should all be able to feel safe in our own home.

Here are some things to keep us safe and comfortable at home!

Don't ever open the door without looking to see who is there first. DING DONG!! Someone is at the door! My mom is home. I ran to the door and fling it open without looking first. What did I do wrong? Well, no matter who may be home, it only takes a second for a stranger to grab a kid who flings the door open…Poof! in the car and gone—never to be seen again!   Let's start over. DING DONG! "Mom!! Someone is at the door! Let me check and see who it is!" "I don't know them, mom!" Now, mom chooses to open the door or ignore the stranger's ring on her doorbell. If an adult is home, let them be the decision makers. If you are home alone, look outside and see who it is, but DON'T OPEN THE DOOR! If they keep ringing and knocking, call the police. If you know them, just ignore them. They will come back later. If someone tries opening the door, go call the police and hide in a safe place until the police arrive.

2. **Don't tell anyone you are home alone!**

The phone rings. You answer it and the adult on the other end asks for your mom or dad. Tell them they aren't interested, or they are in the bathroom, or just hang up without explanation. If you have caller ID, only answer the phone if you know and trust the caller. Don't ever tell a person who calls that your parents aren't home!

Also, you are home alone, you decide to take a selfie lying on the couch with pizza, stating, #homealone #freeatlast! DON'T EVER state on social media you are home alone! If you must be left alone, don't ever tell anyone. If they track you down, it won't be a safe ending.

If you hear a noise outside, don't go outside to check on it! Look out different windows to see if you can find the location of the noise. It may be just an animal. If you see a person lingering on your property, call the police immediately and hide.

Don't ever play outside alone when you are home alone. Being outside alone draws attention to your vulnerability. It is an open door for a predator to grab you or coerce you to go with them.

3.   Don't have friends over when you are home alone. Sometimes, when we are with our friends we don't always make the safest of choices. We sometimes influence each other to do things that aren't always safe in a moment of fun. Being home alone is a very large responsibility and it must be taken seriously. There is a time to play and a time to work. When you are home alone, you are working to stay safe at every moment.

Safe Adults

Children learn to trust adults because they know more and will keep kids safe. In a perfect world, this statement would be true and apply to all adults in society. However, the world is not a perfect place. It is a place filled with imperfect people. There are safe adults, but not all adults

are safe. It is important to figure out which adults are safe because it is important to have adults in your life that you can trust and that can help you anytime. This book won't tell you all the answers, but the following information may teach you how to figure out a safe adult from a non-safe adult.

1.   **Family:**   Family can make you feel very comfortable! In a perfect world, all family members are safe adults. However, this is not always the case. Sometimes, family members cannot be trusted, and it is o.k. to report a family member if they make you feel uncomfortable. If you feel uncomfortable, that is called your gut instinct and you should always trust your gut instinct.

2.   **Friends of Family:** Sometimes family friends are there so much they're like family. This is great if you have safe adults that are friends of your family. If you feel safe around them, then you are blessed with great people in your life! However, if anyone makes you feel uncomfortable, it is necessary to tell a parent or an adult you do trust and feel comfortable around.

3. **Coaches and Teachers:** There are many coaches and teachers that treat their students and team members like their own kids. These teachers and coaches are how all teachers and coaches should be. However, sometimes we

run across a teacher or coach that makes us feel uncomfortable with inappropriate words or actions. Remember, just because they are a teacher or coach, it doesn't  automatically mean they are safe adults. It is o.k. to report a teacher or coach, or any other school authority that may make you feel uncomfortable—even if they tell you not to tell or threaten you if you tell.

4. **Police Officers:** Sometimes there are situations that call for the police to be involved. Most police are trustworthy and will help keep you safe. Every now and then, a person decides to join the police force, not to help but to disguise as a law-abiding person and to get closer to criminal knowledge to use for their own evil plans. This is rare, but it does occur. It is important to remember these tips when working with an officer:

     a.   Make sure the officer is real and has a real badge and a real marked car.

     b.   Make sure the officer is helping you be safe.

     c.   Always report an officer who makes inappropriate comments or touching or makes you uncomfortable in any way.

5.   Doctors:

We go to the doctor when we are sick, or for regular health check-ups. Most doctors are trustworthy, but sometimes bad adults become doctors to prey upon children. Sometimes, we are made to go alone with a doctor. It is best to insist on a parent being in the room. Not all doctors are bad, but it is best not to find out which ones are by going through a bad situation that involves one. In any situation, it is never safe to go off alone with somebody—

even if they have a "safe" job title. Demand a safe adult join you in your visit.

Babysitters/Nannies: Sometimes your parents can't be home with you and they find other people to watch you. It may be just for one night, like a babysitter, or it may be that you have a full-time caregiver, like a nanny. Whatever the scenario, it is important that the person in charge of you is a safe adult that will not harm you in any way. Sometimes, a babysitter or nanny who isn't used to children may react in a violent manner. If this happens, it is important to writ down the date and time and details of the situation and tell your parents or a safe adult. Nobody is allowed to harm children--not even paid employees. If a hired caregiver ever tries to touch you inappropriately, or makes you do things that seem wrong, tell a safe adult. Any adult, even if they were once considered a safe adult by you, can make bad choices that lead us to lose trust in them. If any adult, whether its family, family friends, coaches, teachers, police officers, doctors (or anybody not covered in these topics) ever puts you in a position to do something that makes you uncomfortable, always report it to a safe adult!!

Uncomfortable actions may come from any adult and may include:

Touching you, making you touch them, taking your picture, asking you to remove clothing, trying to kiss you, kissing you, making unwanted compliments, whispering in your ear telling you to keep secrets, calling you sexy, asking you to send pictures, hitting you, pinching you, getting too close, or anything else that might make you comfortable. If you feel uncomfortable (and even if you don't) any of the above actions should be reported. It doesn't matter who did what—REPORT IT! Nobody is above the law. Any touch, anywhere on your body is not ok if it makes you feel nervous or uncomfortable. personal space is important. Any touch on any part of your body where that swimsuit covers is never ok. EVER. REPORT IT IMMEDIATELY! Also, never touch anyone where they wear a swimsuit, even if they tell you to or threaten you. RUN away and tell a safe adult immediately!

Safe Friends & Peers

Friends can make us so happy! It is awesome to hang out with people who have so much in common with us! Having fun with friends is a very important part of life! Having fun is good, but if fun puts you at risk, then it is important to make good choices and stay safe. You can still have fun and be safe!   Follow these guidelines to stay safe when you are with friends! Sometimes we go places with our friends. Follow these rules to stay safe anytime you are with your friends!

1.	**Always be aware of your surroundings!** We know you know where you are, but there is more to knowing where you are than just stating the title of the place. Knowing where you are includes being aware of your surroundings. Are there any suspicious people? Are you aware enough of what's going on around you to realize if somebody is walking up to you, or staring at you? Always be alert enough of your surroundings to be able to react if you notice any alerting situations.

2.   Don't approach or respond to general strangers!
There is no reason you should ever talk to strangers that come up to you and try striking a conversation. The cashier at the store that says hi while they are working is one thing, but some sketchy adults may use excuses like "I lost my dog", "I need your help, come closer", "I'm lost, can you help me find…", "Want a ride?", "Your mom sent me to get you.", and many other clever lies the design to grab you. An adult will not need you to find their dog, help them get unlost, or to keep them company while they drive. Your parents would never send a person you never met to pick you up. It is a trap so don't fall for it. This trap could lead you to serious harm. It could even mean the end of your life.

3.   Know when to report a friend or someone hurting a friend. We love our friends, but sometimes a friend can act in a questionable way and make you feel uncomfortable or leave you harmed. If you have a friend that is physically, mentally, or emotionally harmful to you, or that makes you do things that you don't want to do you need to tell a safe adult. A true friend would never harm you in any way. If a friend ever puts you in a situation that causes harm to you or them, and tells you not to tell anybody, don't listen. Go tell a safe adult. Also, if a friend tells you that someone is harming them and tells you not to tell, tell a safe adult anyway. Secrets between friends don't need to be kept when someone is in danger.

4.	**Mean words can hurt. but don't let them.** Sometimes at school, online or anywhere we go we run across kids that find pleasure in calling you names, saying mean things, threatening you, scaring you, making others gang up on you, and many other situations that make you sad, scared, or uncomfortable. Sometimes, these kids make you feel awful about yourself, make you very sad, and make you feel worthless or stupid.

5.	**YOU ARE NOT DEFINED by their words!** No matter what kids make up and say about you to you or others, it isn't true. Kids do this because they feel bad about something in their own life and it makes them feel good to make somebody else feel bad, too. Please do not ever let another human being make you think badly of yourself. If you find yourself in a bullying situation, ignore the bully and take your problem to a safe adult. If they don't help, take your problem to another safe adult until you get the help you need. Th most important thing to remember is the words they say or write are just words. You control your own life, and you have the power to block this from your mind and not let their meanness affect how you think or feel about yourself. Love yourself, even if somebody else doesn't. They won't always be around, but you will live with yourself forever. LOVE YOURSELF and know that you are not the problem, they are.

 If someone ever tells you to kill yourself, or tell you that you don't matter, or you'd be better off dead, don't get hurt feelings over it. It isn't true. Tell a safe adult and try to get help for your friend. They need it more than you. You are fine. You are perfect, and your life makes a good difference in many other lives around you—regardless of what another person may state in a lie.

Safety Wherever You Go

The world is big, and you need to live life to the fullest! Don't be afraid to go out and do stuff, just be aware of the control you hold in any situation.   Just know what to do in the event an unsafe situation happens! Remember these safe tips!

1.	**If you lose your safe adult in a store:** Sometimes we are standing next to our safe adult in the store and we wander too far, look up and notice they are not near you anymore. That sure can be a scary feeling!! It will be o.k. They will not leave the place without taking you with them. They are still in the store, and they are just as afraid as you are! They want you back safely. Don't just start asking random people for help. Go to a safe store employee and tell them you lost your safe adult. Stay in view and don't ever go back in a room alone with anyone—not even a worker! They will call for your safe adult over the loud speaker. Stay where you are and know that they are on their way to get you back! If a stranger tries to claim you, don't go. Wait patiently for the original safe adult that you arrived with and lost. ONLY GO WITH THEM!!

2.   **If you are on a field trip with school:** Always stay with the group! Don't ever wander off alone--even if you need to use the restroom and think you can sneak back in quickly. It is not ok! If you must use the restroom tell a chaperone or teacher and go with an approved group. Even if you are finished, wait for the rest of your group and go back together! Never leave anyone behind or go alone! Sometimes, you may wander off into

a daydream while the teacher is giving instructions on where to be and when, ASK what you missed and make sure you know what is happening, so you don't get lost by being at the wrong place at the wrong time.

3.   **If you are ever grabbed by a stranger.** Scream, kick, fight, holler, yell, and draw as much attention as you can to yourself! Try to get away. Use your elbows, feet, nails, hands, or anything you have to fight the person off of you. It is o.k. to use violence to protect yourself from a harmful stranger!! Do whatever you can do to get away

and reach a safe adult!! If nobody is around, do your best to be as loud as you can and to get away. Even if you don't see anyone, it doesn't mean they can't hear you or help you if you run to them.

4.   **Walking:** Sometimes we walk to school or home from school, to a friend's house, a library, or any other place we want to visit!

a.   **It is better to walk with at least 1 person, but if you must walk alone, be safe!** Know your surroundings, look out for people and be aware if there is a person string or heading toward to.

b.   **Be ready to run.**   If someone is suspicious—run and be obvious to as many people around you as you can. Run towards people, not into a hidden place.

c.   **Never take a shortcut through woods or out of view!**   If you run into the woods, chances are the person you are running from can get you and nobody would see it.

d.   **Patterns are made** if you walk at the same place and time every day. Be on the lookout for people watching you. You are letting

them know when they can grab

you daily if you don't change up

your times of walking.

Conclusion for Kids:

Some of the information in this book is scary. It is o.k. if you feel scared. Talk to a safe adult about how you feel. The world can be scary at times, but now you know what to do to stay safe! Doesn't that feel good? I bet you feel strong and brave, now! Always remember what you learned and use it every day! Please also share your knowledge with your friends, too! You will be helping keep them safe! Thank you for learning that Knowledge is Control!

Safety Tips for Parents

- Have a family computer, not a computer in your child's room.   This computer will be evident to everyone and not a secretive device.

- Observe the people in your child's life. Make sure that if any teacher, priest, coach, event leader etc. gives gifts or takes a special interest in your child, that you confront the issue and never let your child alone with them.

- Never run into a public place and leave your children in the car. Even if they are watching each other— it isn't safe. It only takes 1 minute for them to disappear.

- Have a scream-fest!! This lets your kids practice their best screams! Practicing screaming is great because it primes the throat in the event they ever need to scream—they will know how!!

- Always talk to your child. Know about their day, people they communicate with, places they go, and ask them specific questions and let them know you are a safe adult to talk to about anything. If your child wakes you up with a nightmare. Listen. Sometimes real-life occurrences cause nightmares, bedwetting, or other nighttime concerns. Let them talk and ask them how it relates in their real life.

- Always know where your kids should be at any given time and have a communication plan to contact them anytime you want/need.

- Tell your children that although it isn't ok to be rude to people, it is ok if they are hurting you, or making you feel uncomfortable. Self-defense is important!

- Always be involved in the activities your kid(s) participate in. Know the team leaders/coaches, etc., and never let your child be alone with them outside the group.

- If your child hears a news story that scares them, have a talk with them about it. Don't tell them it didn't happen but tell them that sometimes things happen that's scary and that's normal in life.

- Talk about secrets, vs. surprises. Secrets are dangerous things that they are told not to repeat, even though they should. Surprises are fun things that everyone finds out about soon-like a party!

- Never let your child walk to a friend's house alone and be aware of all the Registered Sex Offenders in the area you live and beyond! Check the list for all areas your child visits on a regular basis!

Conclusion for the Parents

This book is not meant to cause harmful fears, but it is meant to bring awareness to the dangers that surround us each day. We believe that knowledge is control, and once you are aware of potential hazards, you can have a plan to prevent and react to such situations.

Too many times, adults are afraid to scare children, so they don't really give the really important details. This can be more of a danger than giving the scary information because it leads the child through a false bliss that keeps them from saving themselves from cautious scenarios. If the children don't know something bad or scary could happen, they don't know the situation exists, therefore they don't know how to handle it if it should occur. Not having a plan is scary but being educated to risks and solutions gives the children a sense of control and confidence.

The truth is, the world is filled with crazy people, and many of them prey on children. We cannot stop these people from being the way they are, but we can protect our children from people like that. Since we cannot always be with them, this book was made to give the children the knowledge to stay safe, even when they are alone.

We spend every minute of our lives being the best parent we can be and keeping our children safe from all the dangers in the world. Thank you for letting us help you keep your kids safe.

www.ingramcontent.com/pod-product-compliance
Lightning Source LLC
Chambersburg PA
CBHW061645130726

47996CB00003B/1464